THE SUPER SCIENCE BOOK OF FORCES

Jerry Wellington

Wooden Life

A seesaw is not a seesaw
With no one at the other end
Just an inert piece of wood
Going nowhere
With me sat
Feeling
Foolish
Pretending
It's meant to go like this.

When at last
Someone clambers on the other end
I grip the metal-smelling handles,
Flecked with red,
So tightly
My bones shine white through my skin
As the piece of wood
Whose every knot my eyes have explored
Flies into life.

My piece of wood
Breathes in the wind
Revived as a seesaw
Not just a dead
Silent plank
Split from a tree that once
Was as alive and swinging
As a
Seesaw.

by Lizzie Lewis

Illustrations by Frances Lloyd

Thomson Learning
New York

Titles in the Super Science series

Energy
The Environment
Forces
Life Processes
Materials
Light

Our Bodies
Rocks and Soils
Sound
Space
Time
Weather

First published in the
United States in 1994 by
Thomson Learning
115 Fifth Avenue
New York, NY 10003

First published in 1994 by Wayland (Publishers) Ltd.

Library of Congress Cataloging-in-Publication Data
Wellington, J. J. (Jerry J.)
   The super science book of forces / Jerry Wellington;
illustrations by Frances Lloyd.
        p.   cm. – (Super science series)
   Includes bibliographic references and index.
   ISBN 1-56847-223-4
   1. Force and energy – Juvenile literature. 2. Power
(Mechanics) – Juvenile literature. [1. Force and energy.
2. Power (Mechanics)] I. Lloyd, Frances, ill. II. Title.
III. Series: Super science.
QC73.4.W45   1994
531 – dc20   94-4558

Printed in Italy

Series Editor: Jim Kerr
Designer: Loraine Hayes Design

Picture acknowledgments
Illustrations by Frances Lloyd
Cover illustration by Martin Gordon

Photograph acknowledgments:
The Publishers would like to thank the following for
providing the pictures used in this book: Action Plus 5
(Chris Barry), 6 top, 8 (both Richard Francis), 11 (Chris
Barry), 12 (Richard Francis), 19 (Chris Barry), 20 top, 20
bottom (Chris Barry); Chapel Studios 10; Bruce Coleman 7
(Kim Taylor); Eye Ubiquitous 13, 15, 23 (Nick Wiseman), 29
(Keith Sutton); Michael Holford 22; Science Photo Library
14 right (Marcello Bertinetti) Tony Stone 16 (Paul
McKelvey), 16 (Peter Lamberti), 25 top (W. Rudolph);
Quadrant 21 (Luca Badoer), 25 bottom, 26, 28; Wayland
Picture Library 6 bottom, 9, 14 left, 24.

CONTENTS

PUSHES AND PULLS

You can see forces being used wherever you look. This book is all about forces – big ones and small ones – and how they are used.

Here are some drawings of people using forces.
▼

Look at the forces being used in each picture. In every one there is either a *push* or a *pull* involved.

The woman is pulling back the string on her bow, ready to let it go so that it pushes an arrow forward. The hammer is pushing down on the nail, forcing it into the wood. The person opening the paint can is using the screwdriver as a lever: pushing down on the screwdriver's handle causes the other end to push up on the lid. The man pulling a sled is using a force to pull it over the snow. The woman pushing the lawn roller is using a force to flatten her lawn. All the people here are using forces to do a job for them.

Every day of your life you use forces in some way or other: walking to school, opening a door, lifting books, kicking a ball, or just standing up. Where do these forces come from?

◄ A person wearing a parachute does not fall quickly but sails slowly toward the earth. What forces are at work here? The parachutist's weight pulls him or her toward the center of the earth. Weight is one kind of force, probably the most common force of all. However, another force is acting in the opposite direction. It is the force caused by air resistance on the parachute. This slows down a parachutist and stops him or her from plunging toward the earth at great speed.

This book tells you how forces can be used to:
● slow things down.
● speed things up.
● help things change direction.
● change the shape or size of some objects.

BIG AND SMALL

Forces are either pushes or pulls. Some forces are very big. This weight lifter needs a large force to lift a weight over his shoulders and then hold it there. He is pushing up on the bar, while the bar is being pulled down by the earth's gravity. His upward push and the bar's downward weight are balanced. ▼

▲ During a tug of war, each team does its best to pull the other over. They are using as much force as they can, but at the moment the two pulls are equal. What would happen if one side suddenly started pulling with a stronger force than the other?

People can produce large forces, but machines can be used to produce even bigger pushes and pulls. Some machines can provide enormous forces that are very useful to us. They can be used to pull a boat out of a river or to lift heavy weights. ▼

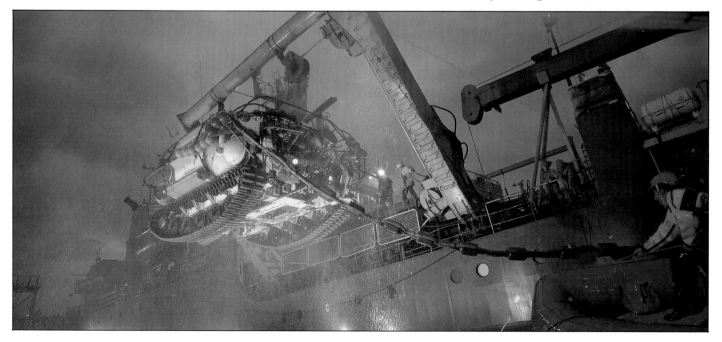

Some forces that we ▶ see and use are very small. An insect floating on water is very light in weight, but it still has to be held up by a small force. This comes from a kind of "skin" on the water's surface called surface tension.

WOW!
Several weight lifters have been able to lift over five times their body weight.

Scientists find out how things work ▶ by taking measurements. In the metric system, force, which is the same as weight, is measured in newtons. Mass, which is the amount of material in an object, is measured in kilograms. This can be confusing because in practice we use kilograms as a meaure of weight in the same way as pounds. This is because on Earth mass and weight are directly related.

In the English or American system we use pounds to measure force and slugs to measure mass. This book shows a number of objects and their sizes given in newtons. Just think of 1 pound as being equal to roughly 5 newtons, or a medium-sized apple as about 1 newton.

Type of Force	Force in Newtons
Weight of an apple	1
Force needed to peel a banana	1
Friction on a rolling soccer ball	2
Squeeze needed to break an egg	50
Force needed to kick a soccer ball	100
Your weight	400-500
Force of a train's engine	10,000
Force of a rocket's engines	1,000,000

USING FORCES

What can forces do?

Forces can do lots of ▶ things that can be very useful to us. They can bend, twist, squeeze, or stretch things. You can try this with a piece of sponge or a lump of modeling clay.

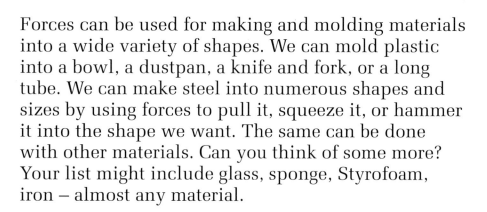

Forces can be used for making and molding materials into a wide variety of shapes. We can mold plastic into a bowl, a dustpan, a knife and fork, or a long tube. We can make steel into numerous shapes and sizes by using forces to pull it, squeeze it, or hammer it into the shape we want. The same can be done with other materials. Can you think of some more? Your list might include glass, sponge, Styrofoam, iron – almost any material.

◀ Forces also can be used to speed things up or slow them down. Later in this book we look at starting and stopping. Very often we use a force to make things go around and around in circles. A stone on the end of a string can be whirled around in a circle. The force needed to do this comes from the person pulling on the string. If the person were to let go, the stone would fly off in a straight line. Hammer throwers competing in athletics use a similar technique.

Ramps and levers

Two of the most efficient uses of 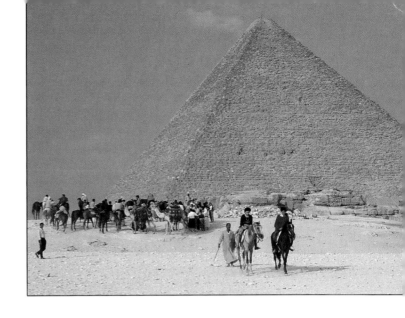 forces have been used for centuries: ramps and levers. Ramps, or inclined planes, were probably used to build Stonehenge in England and the Egyptian pyramids shown in the picture. Less force is needed to drag heavy stones into position than to lift them straight up.

Heavy objects can also be moved into position using a lever. This can be a long piece of wood or metal resting on a support called a pivot. A smaller force on the long side of the lever can be turned into a much larger force on the short side – very useful for shifting huge boulders.

The ancient Greek scientist Archimedes once said: "Give me a lever in the right place and I will move the world." But he would also need something to rest the lever on: a pivot.

SLIPPING AND SLIDING

Try sliding this book along the top of a table or bench. What happens? If you push it and let go, it soon stops. To keep it going you have to keep on pushing it. Your pushing force is working against another force in the opposite direction. This opposite force is called friction.

Friction occurs whenever two things rub against each other. Rub your hands together and you feel heat from friction. Pedal a bike and you have to work hard against the friction between the different parts of it and the friction between the road and the tires.

Rub your hands together when they are completely dry. Then try rubbing them together when they are wet and soapy. What difference do you notice?

◄ Very often we try to make friction as small as possible. You can reduce friction on a bike by rubbing oil on the parts that rub together. The oil on your chain and on the wheel axles helps to reduce the friction. Oil gets between any two surfaces that rub together and makes a thin, greasy layer. Making a slippery layer between two things that normally rub against each other is called lubrication.

◄ The best time of year for natural lubrication is winter, if it is icy and snowy. If you go sledding down a hill, there is very little friction to slow you down. If you go skiing, the skis slide over the snow and ice. There is far less friction than if you tried to ski on grass or soil, or even on the plastic matting of a dry ski slope. Most skiers put wax on the bottom of their skis to reduce the friction even more.

These are people in a bobsled. Bobsleds go down ▶ special runs like the ones you may have seen on televised bobsled races (as in the Olympics). There is almost no friction between the bobsled and the slope, so they reach speeds of 65 miles per hour or more.

Don't forget, though, that friction also can be very useful. In fact, we couldn't live without it. Imagine living in a world without friction. You wouldn't be able to walk or ride a bike without friction between the pavement and the soles of your shoes or the bicycle tires.

STOPPING AND STARTING

In order for a ball to move, it needs ▶ a force to get it going. You can get it moving with a hit or kick. In fact, everything requires some force to cause it to move. The ball gradually slows down and stops – it will not keep moving forever. This is because on earth there are other forces slowing it down or changing its direction. The resistance, or friction, in the air, together with gravity pulling it down, causes the ball to gradually stop moving.

Sir Isaac Newton, a famous scientist of the seventeenth century, was the first person to realize that a moving object will continue moving in a straight line if there is no force acting on it. In life on Earth, we never see this happen. But imagine a world with no friction and no gravity. A cannonball fired from a cannon would keep on going into outer space, where there is very little friction, until it hit something. ▼

This table shows some ▶ different speeds. Even the plane has a type of friction working against it, called air resistance.

How does your speed compare with these? How fast can you run?

Airplane	800-900 feet per second
Fast car	150-175 feet per second
Cheetah	90-100 feet per second
Olympic sprinter	30-35 feet per second
Marathon runner	8-9 feet per second

Once things are moving it takes a ▲ force to stop them. If you are in a car and it crashes, your body will keep on moving. If you're wearing a seat belt it will stop you. If not, you keep moving until another force stops you. This could be your impact on the car's windshield.

It takes a long time for a fast-moving car to come to a halt just by using its brakes. Look at the stopping distances for a car traveling at various speeds.

Speed of car	Total stopping distance
30 mph	75 feet
50 mph	175 feet
70 mph	315 feet

You can see that it takes more than 300 feet for a car traveling at 70 miles per hour to come to a halt. It can take even longer to stop if the road is wet, oily, or icy.

13

OTHER FORCES

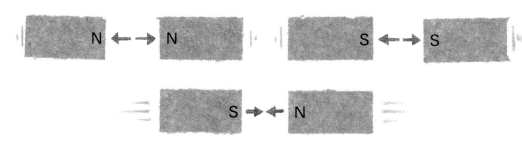

The two most common forces that we come across every day are friction and gravity. A child coming down a slide is pulled down by the force of gravity. But he or she is slowed down a little by friction. ▼

There are other important forces that we sometimes ▲ see in action. One is magnetic force. The two magnets in this drawing are pushing each other apart. The two ends, or poles, of the magnets facing each other are of the same kind. They are both north poles. Suppose you turned them both around. They would still push each other apart. How can you make them attract each other? Two magnets attract each other when the two poles facing each other are different: a south pole facing a north pole.

▲ Forces from magnets can be very useful. Some special trains use magnetic force to hold the train in midair just above a single rail. This helps the train to travel with much less friction than an ordinary train. These magnetic levitation trains are used in Japan and in England.

Holding a magnet in midair

Place two magnets together with two poles of the same kind close to each other. Then slowly raise the end of one so that it is just above the same pole of the other. You should be able to get the second magnet to stay in midair.

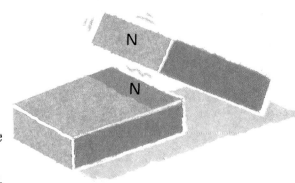

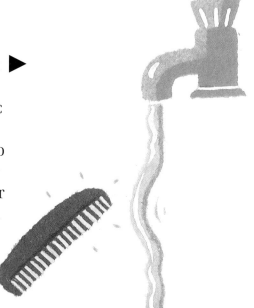

◀ Magnetic force also can be made using a special kind of magnet called an electromagnet. An electric current is passed through a coil of wire wrapped around a piece of magnetic material such as iron. Huge electromagnets are sometimes used to pick up cars in scrap yards. When the current is switched on, the iron bar becomes magnetic and can lift a steel car. When the current is switched off, it is no longer a magnet and the car is dropped.

Another very important ▶ force is caused by static electricity. Rub a plastic comb on your sleeve, and then hold it close to a gentle stream of water from a faucet. The water bends toward the comb. An electrostatic force is working here.

Rub two balloons together. They should then push each other apart. If you rub a plastic comb or pen on your sleeve, the comb or pen can be used to pick up small pieces of paper. These are examples of electrostatic forces.

THE EARTH'S PULL

Here is a man falling ▶ through the air, but he won't hit the ground at high speed. A long piece of very strong elastic rope is tied to his body. He will bounce up and down a few times on the end of the rope and then come to rest. This is a new sport called bungee jumping. The bungee jumper's life depends on the force of gravity being balanced by the tension in the rope.

◀ A much older sport is skydiving. People jump from a plane and fall through the air without a parachute for a short time. At first they speed up, or accelerate, very quickly. After a time the friction of the air, or air resistance, stops them from accelerating and they reach a steady speed. This is a very fast speed, about 100 miles per hour, so very soon the sky divers open their parachutes. These have much more air resistance than the sky diver's body alone so he or she is slowed down to a safe speed before landing.

Dropping objects

Drop several different solid objects to the ground, all from the same height to make it a fair test (6 feet, for example). You could use a peanut, a marble, and a baseball, a tennis ball, and a golf ball. What do you expect to happen? Which one reaches the ground first?

A famous scientist named Galileo was the first to ▶ realize that objects of the same shape, but with different weights, fall to the ground at the same speed. According to one story, he dropped steel cannonballs with different weights from the Leaning Tower of Pisa, in Italy, and measured the time each took to fall to the ground. They both reached the ground at the same time.

▲ Sir Isaac Newton was the first to say that gravity doesn't act only near the earth. There is gravity from other planets, the stars, and everywhere in the universe. It is the sun's gravity that keeps the planets in their orbits, or circular paths, and keeps the earth going around the sun. The earth's gravity keeps the moon traveling in its orbit around the earth. The pull of the earth on the moon keeps it traveling in this curved orbit. The same thing happens with a satellite in orbit around the earth. The earth's gravity keeps the satellite moving in a curved path around the earth. Without the earth's gravity, the satellite would shoot off in a straight line into space.

WOW!
Did you know that your weight is slightly different at different places on the earth? At the top of Mount Everest your weight is about half a pound less than at sea level. At the equator your weight is about one pound (5 apples' worth) less than at the North Pole. The farther you are from the center of the earth, the less you weigh.

PRESSURE POINTS

Sitting on a bed of ▶ nails looks very painful. It is painful to sit on just one nail. But on this bed of hundreds of nails, this man has spread his weight over a large number of points. The pressure from each nail is not enough to break his skin.

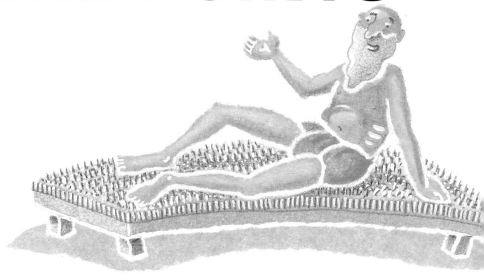

Another place where it is useful to spread out your weight is on deep snow. Special snow shoes can spread someone's weight over a large area, to stop them from sinking down into the snow. The pressure on the snow is less because the force downward (the person's weight) acts over a larger area of snow.

Spreading the force

Take two coins and two pieces of modeling clay. Press one coin into the first piece with the flat side down.

Now press the other coin into the second piece, this time with the edge down. Which sinks more easily?

The coin on its edge is easier to press down. The coin's edge has a much smaller area than its face. The smaller the area, the bigger the pressure made by your hand pushing down.

There are times when it is helpful to spread weight over a large area: walking on snow, crawling across thin, dangerous ice, or clambering over a fragile roof. Sometimes, however, the opposite is needed. If you go ice skating, your weight is concentrated on a thin, narrow blade. This puts much more pressure on the ice than a flat shoe would. The pressure helps to melt the ice into a thin film of water so that you glide over the surface. ▶

WOW!

Have you heard about the elephant and the stiletto heel? The pressure on the ground from a high heel shoe can be as big as the pressure from an elephant's foot. A woman is obviously lighter, but her weight is concentrated on a much smaller area. The heavier elephant has its weight spread over four large, flat feet.

SPORTS FORCES

Every sport involves ▶ forces of one kind or another. Some sports, such as football and Sumo wrestling, involve very large pushing and pulling forces.

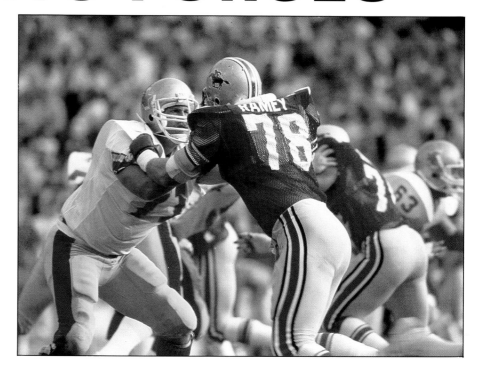

Some of the forces used in games like tennis and golf may not seem particularly big. But if they are studied closely, using high-speed photography, you see that the force of a tennis racket or a golf club is actually quite strong.

◀ High-speed photos show that the ball is flattened when hit. Balls are squashed for a fraction of a second, but they soon get back to their regular shape and then move away at a very high speed: sometimes more than 100 miles per hour.

Once a ball is flying through the air, the way it travels depends on whether it is spinning. A golf ball, a football, a tennis ball, and a baseball all can be given some spin, which makes them follow a curved path through the air. Soccer players also can do this by kicking one side of the ball to give it sidespin. This is sometimes called a banana kick.

In some sports it is very important ▶ to keep the force of friction as low as possible. Look at this ski jumper. As she comes down the ramp before takeoff, she bends down and keeps her hands behind her back. This reduces the air resistance, or drag, on her body. After leaving the ramp she angles her body upward so that the air lifts her up and she glides through the air. She must lean at exactly the right angle. What do you think would happen if she leaned too far forward or too far back?

Another sport where air resistance ▶ must be as low as possible is car racing. The wing, or airfoil, on the back of the car helps to reduce the drag.

WOW!
Do you know why golf balls have little dents, or dimples, in them? A dimpled ball has much less drag on it than a ball with a smooth surface. This means that it travels much farther when it is struck.

BUILDINGS AND BRIDGES

Throughout history, man has built a great number of structures to suit his various needs. You see structures around you every day. The pyramids and Stonehenge are ancient structures; large bridges and skyscrapers are newer structures.

Engineers must understand how ▶ forces affect structures, so that they remain standing under all kinds of conditions, even earthquakes. One of the oldest structures built by man is the stone arch. It is used in walls, doorways, gateways, and bridges. Arches are very strong because the stones in the arch press against one another and hold each other in place. Stone arches will stay up even if there is no cement between the stones. Some arches, built thousands of years ago by the ancient Greeks and Romans, are still standing.

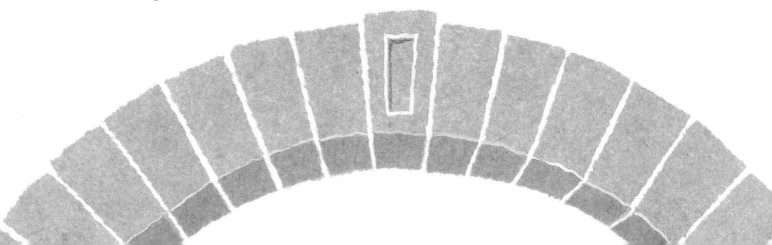

▲ The drawings below show three common types of bridges. You may have seen bridges using each of these kinds of structures. In a suspension bridge like the one above, cables pull the two towers downward and inward. Bridges are built so that they can hold the weight of cars or trains pressing down on them. But they also have to be designed to stand up to forces from either side. These are the forces of the wind blowing into them and the water crashing against them. If it cannot withstand these forces, a bridge will collapse.

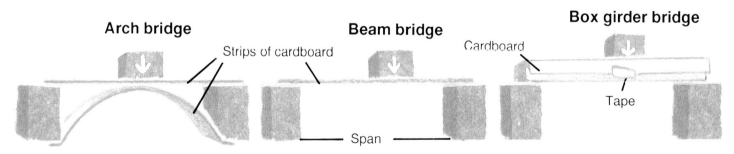

Arch bridge Strips of cardboard

Beam bridge Span

Box girder bridge Cardboard Tape

Making Bridges

Compare the strength of three different types of bridges using heavy cardboard and weights. Make a beam bridge, an arch bridge, and a box girder bridge as the drawing shows. Make the span (the length) of the bridge the same for each one.

Which type do you think will be the strongest? Test your prediction. Try widening the span to see what happens.

FORCES IN WATER

Why do some things float in water and others sink? Wood, cork, Styrofoam, wax, and ice all float. A piece of lead or steel will sink, as will a stone or a brick.

According to an ancient story, a ▶ Greek named Archimedes once got in the bathtub, saw the water level go up, and realized that an upward force, an upthrust, was pushing up on him. He shouted *"Eureka!,"* Greek for "I have found it!" He realized that as he lowered himself farther into the bathtub and pushed water aside and upward, more and more force was pushing up on him.

◀ His discovery became known as Archimedes' principle. It explains why a steel ship carrying heavy cargo will float although a steel block will sink. A steel ship is shaped so that it pushes aside a lot of water. This pushed aside water, like the water in Archimedes' bathtub, pushes up on the ship and balances its weight.

◀ People can just about float in a swimming pool or the sea. But there is one unusual place called the Dead Sea (in Jordan, in the Middle East) where people can float very easily. The Dead Sea is extremely salty, and this gives a much larger upthrust on a person than ordinary seawater.

If a ship is loaded with a great deal ▶ of cargo it will sink very low into the water. In the nineteenth century, many greedy shipowners loaded their ships with so much cargo that they barely floated, and sometimes they sank in storms. Then, in 1876, Samuel Plimsoll introduced special lines that had to be marked on the sides of all ships. It is now against the law to overload a ship so that the water comes above these plimsoll lines, or load lines.

HIGH-SPEED FORCES

Human beings are capable of producing very large pushes and pulls. A strong man can lift a weight of more than 200 pounds over his head. But to produce really large forces, engines are needed.

▲ One of the most common engines we use is the car engine. Its full name is the internal combustion engine because it burns a fuel, such as gasoline, at the heart of the engine. The main parts of a car engine are the cylinders. These are below the silver object in the picture, and are where the driving force of a car comes from. Inside each cylinder, a mixture of air and gas is sucked in. A spark ignites the mixture and produces a tremendous force like an explosion. This forces the piston down at a high speed. As the piston goes down it turns a rod or shaft around and around very quickly. This movement goes through a system of gears and eventually turns the wheels of the car. It sounds complicated, but just remember that the main driving force comes from a fuel that "explodes" inside the cylinders.

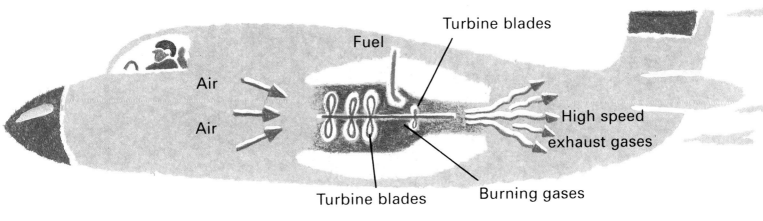

Fuel

Turbine blades

Air

Air

Turbine blades

Burning gases

High speed exhaust gases

▲ Car engines can produce forces of several thousand newtons. A train engine can produce forces of 10,000 newtons. An even more powerful engine is the jet engine.

Have you ever blown up a balloon and then let it go so that it flies around? A jet engine works in the same way. Inside the engine, a mixture of air and jet fuel is set on fire, which rushes at high speed out of the back of the engine. At the same time, the engine, and the plane attached to it, is pushed forward.

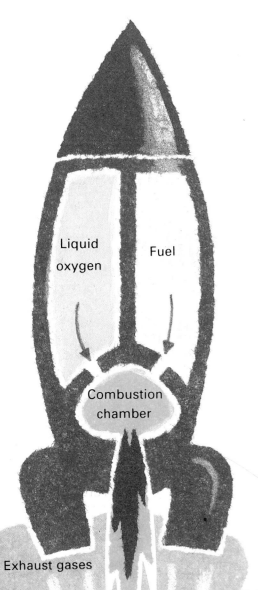

Liquid oxygen

Fuel

Combustion chamber

Exhaust gases

◄ A rocket engine works in the same way, except that rockets have to fly in space where there is no air. This means that they must carry their own supply of oxygen so that the rocket fuel can burn. The oxygen on board mixes with the rocket fuel and burns in a special combustion chamber. The hot gases zoom out of the back of the rocket through a nozzle. As the gases rush backward, the rocket is pushed forward.

The force of a rocket engine can be as much as 1,000,000 newtons: that's like 1,000 strong people all pushing at once!

BALANCING ACT

How can a very heavy person and a light child balance each other on a seesaw? You can see the answer in this drawing. ▶

The man is very close to the balance point, or pivot. The girl is much farther away. They both have the same turning effect, so they balance. A tall crane with a long arm works in the same way. The load on the end of the crane is balanced by a heavy weight at the other end.

▲ Balance of forces is necessary in many areas of life, including some sports, building work, and industry. This photo shows people on a yacht working hard to keep the boat from overturning. They are leaning out over the side. This increases the turning effect of their weight and helps to balance the strong force of the wind on the sail trying to turn the boat the other way. If they lean out far enough, they can stop the boat from capsizing.

A major consideration when ▶
creating designs is to make sure that
things stay upright. If you push this
doll to one side, it does not topple
over, but comes back up again. It is
designed to be very stable. The doll
has a large, heavy base. Racing cars are
designed in the same way. They need
to be stable so that when they take a
corner at high speed they don't
overturn. A racing car has a very wide
base (the distance between the wheels)
and its weight is low down. We say
that it has a low center of gravity.

◀ Things with a high
center of gravity topple
over very easily. A
person standing up
in a rowboat and a
unicyclist both have a
high center of gravity,
and are very unstable.

A balancing trick

You will need a potato,
two forks, a small cup,
and a small coin. Stick
the forks and the coin in
the potato as this
drawing shows.

Hold the cup and rest
the coin on the very
edge of it. What
happens?

GLOSSARY

Acceleration   Any change in the speed or the direction that an object is moving.

Air resistance   The force slowing an object down when it travels through the air. It is a type of friction.

Compressed   Squashed into a smaller volume.

Drag   Another name for air resistance.

Electromagnet   A magnet that is created in a coil of wire as a result of a current of electricity passing through it.

Friction   The force that acts between two objects that are touching and which acts against the movement of one surface over another.

Gravity   The pull of one object on another. This force is only obvious with massive objects, such as the earth, which pulls objects down toward its surface.

Lubrication   Adding a substance, such as oil, to the space between two surfaces to make them slippery or smooth and therefore reduce friction between them.

Newton (N)   The metric unit for measuring the force known as weight. In practice, the gram or kilogram (1,000 grams) is used to measure weight. In the United States, weight is measured in pounds and ounces. There are about 4 ½ newtons in 1 pound.

Orbit   The curved path that the moon or a satellite follows around the earth, or a planet follows around the sun.

Pivot   The point around which a seesaw or lever turns.

Speed   The distance traveled by a moving object in a certain period of time.

Surface tension   The "skin" on the surface of water that allows some things to lie on the surface and not sink.

Thrust   A forward force produced, for example, by the engine of an airplane.

Turning effect   The turning effect of a force depends on the size of the force and how far it is from the balance point or pivot. In science, the turning effect of a force is called its "moment." The farther the force is from the pivot, the bigger the moment.

Upthrust   The upward force on an object, such as a ship, when it is in water.

Weight   The pull of gravity on an object.

BOOKS TO READ

Bardon, Keith. *Exploring Forces and Structures.* Milwaukee: Raintree Steck-Vaughn, 1992.

Dunn, Andrew. *Bridges.* Structures. New York: Thomson Learning, 1993.

Dunn, Andrew. *Lifting by Levers.* How Things Work. New York: Thomson Learning, 1993.

Dunn, Andrew. *The Power of Pressure.* How Things Work. New York: Thomson Learning, 1993.

Friedhoffer, Robert. *Forces, Motion, and Energy.* Scientific Magic. New York: Franklin Watts, 1992.

Haslam, Andrew. *Building.* Make It Work! Science. New York: Thomson Learning, 1994.

Lafferty, Peter. *Archimedes.* Pioneers of Science. New York: Bookwright Press, 1991.

McTavish, Douglas. *Galileo.* Pioneers of Science. New York: Bookwright Press, 1991.

McTavish, Douglas. *Isaac Newton.* Pioneers of Science. New York: Bookwright, 1990.

Peacock, Graham. *Forces.* Science Activities. New York: Thomson Learning, 1994.

Science in Action: Projects in Physics. North Bellmore, NY: Marshall Cavendish, 1993.

Stockley, C. *Dictionary of Physics.* Tulsa, OK: EDC Publishing, 1988.

Taylor, Barbara. *Forces and Movement.* Science Starters. Franklin Watts, 1990.

Vancleave, Janice. *Physics for Every Kid: 101 Easy Experiments in Motion, Heat, Light, Machines, and Sound.* New York: John Wiley & Sons, 1991.

INDEX